Biography.

Tom Streissguth

Lerner Publications Company
Minneapolis

To Marie-Christine, my own ambassador from France

Copyright © 2002 by Tom Streissguth

Lerner Publications Company
A division of Lerner Publishing Group
241 First Avenue North
Minneapolis, MN 55401 U.S.A.

Website address: www.lernerbooks.com

Library of Congress Cataloging-in-Publication Data

Streissguth, Thomas, 1958–
    Benjamin Franklin / by Tom Streissguth.
        p.   cm. — (A&E biography)
    Includes bibliographical references and index.
    ISBN: 0–8225–4997–2 (lib. bdg. : alk. paper)
    1. Franklin, Benjamin, 1706–1790—Juvenile literature. 2. Statesmen—
United States—Biography—Juvenile literature. 3. Inventors—United
States—Biography—Juvenile literature. 4. Scientists—United States—
Biography—Juvenile literature. 5. Printers—United States—Biography—
Juvenile literature. [1. Franklin, Benjamin, 1706–1790. 2. Statesmen.
3. Printers. 4. Scientists.] I. Title. II. Biography (Lerner Publications
Company)
E302.6.F8 S9 2002
973.7'092—dc21   2002000579

Manufactured in the United States of America
1 2 3 4 5 6 – JR – 07 06 05 04 03 02

CONTENTS

Although Benjamin Franklin grew up in a humble home, he charmed French aristocrats.

Chapter **ONE**

THE FAMOUS DOCTOR FRANKLIN

ONE **FEBRUARY DAY IN 1778, A HORSE-DRAWN** coach drew up to the immense iron gates of Versailles, the grand palace of Louis XVI, king of France. The palace guards stood smartly at attention as a portly old gentleman climbed down from the coach. At seventy-two, he moved gingerly. The guards recognized him immediately and admitted him to the palace, where he was taken down a seemingly endless hall to the reception room.

There members of the court were waiting together for the arrival of the king. They dressed in high style in large, white-powdered wigs and colorful finery. The men wore coats richly embellished with lace and gold trim. The women's elaborate silk dresses swept across the floor. The portly old gentleman was simply clad, however, in an unembroidered brown velvet coat. He had bought a wig for this occasion, but he'd decided not to wear it. It didn't sit well on his head. Instead he had donned a coonskin cap he had acquired in the British colonies in North America, where he lived. His face was rounded, his forehead high. Behind his spectacles, his eyes were alert and cool.

Then Louis appeared. He looked most magnificent of all, as befitted a king. His sword glittered, as did the priceless gems on his white fur robe. Everyone

Louis XVI of France draped in an exquisite robe amidst the riches of Versailles

took a deep bow. The old gentleman took his bow as well and politely removed his humble cap.

Although Benjamin Franklin looked unimpressive among these French aristocrats, he had in fact already deeply impressed them. They knew him as "Doctor Franklin," a man renowned for his knowledge of natural philosophy (as science was called). Franklin's experiments with electricity—and especially with lightning—were known around the world. But it was not as a scientist that Franklin stood before the court. He was an ambassador, sent by American leaders who had begun a revolt against the rule of Great Britain.

Franklin had been living in a house between Versailles and Paris, the French capital. He had met as many important people as possible, encouraging them to send money, arms, and supplies to aid the American Revolution. He had also been negotiating two treaties that would make France an official ally of the colonists. France was a longtime rival of Great Britain. Both nations had built forts and established colonies in North America. Decades of war between the two had left the British in control of much of that continent.

Franklin's attire may have been calculated to remind the French that he was an emissary from the "New World," a place they romanticized as wild and pure. "His clothing was rustic, his bearing simple but dignified, his language direct, his hair unpowdered," wrote one French nobleman. "It was as though [he] had been brought by magic into our effeminate and slavish age."

France was astir, wrote the same Frenchman, with "a universal love of liberty." Franklin seemed to embody this ideal. When diplomat John Adams stayed in Paris, he observed, "There was scarcely a peasant or a citizen . . . who did not consider [Benjamin Franklin] a friend to human kind." Franklin himself wrote, "'Tis a common observation here, that our Cause is the Cause of all Mankind, and that we are fighting for their Liberty in defending our own."

If the Americans won their war, they would begin a democracy and no longer be ruled by King George III. It is possible that Louis XVI wondered whether other monarchs might be threatened if the Americans succeeded. Certainly he questioned whether France could afford to invest in America's risky war. Regardless, Louis did sign the treaties on February 6, 1778. Franklin had won a major victory for the colonists.

"He seized the lightning from the sky, and the scepter from the tyrants," one Frenchman said of Franklin. But Franklin had once been a fiercely loyal subject of the British king. His earlier life held no sign that he would seize anything, in fact. He came from a humble working family—the Franklins of Ecton, England.

FROM THE OLD WORLD TO THE NEW

Franklin's ancestors had lived in Ecton for many generations. Like their fellow citizens, they were bound by law to remain in their homeland. After the discovery

In 1778 a well-known French economist named A. R. J. Turgot said that Franklin "seized the lightning from the sky, and the scepter from the tyrants." This illustration, based on Turgot's phrase, appeared in French newspapers in the late 1770s.

of the New World, however, England's leaders began to encourage citizens to emigrate to America. As colonists, they could send lumber, furs, tobacco, silver, and gold back to the mother country.

In 1683 Benjamin's father, Josiah Franklin, took his family to the New World to seek his fortune. He and his wife, Anne, and their three children landed in the busy port city of Boston in Massachusetts Bay Colony. Josiah was a dyer of textiles, but dyers were not in demand in Boston. Josiah decided to become a chandler—a maker of candles and soap.

In 1688 Anne Franklin died after giving birth to her seventh child. Josiah then took a second wife, Abiah Folger. Their eighth child (Josiah's tenth boy) was born on January 17, 1706. They named him Benjamin after Josiah's brother, a devout Christian man. In all, Abiah had ten children.

Together with many of Josiah's children from his first marriage, the family crowded into a small house warmed with fireplaces and lit by candles. The house must have bustled with people and activity. For several

An illustration of Benjamin Franklin's birthplace in Boston

years, Uncle Benjamin lived with them. As Josiah became a respected member of the community, many
people, including Boston's leaders, came to the house
to seek his advice. And Josiah always seemed to have
guests for dinner. According to Benjamin, Josiah
thought lively, adult conversation would "improve the
minds of his children."

Benjamin loved to run in the streets of Boston and
swim in the Charles River. One day, Benjamin led a
group of boys in stealing some quarried stone intended for a new house. The boys then built a small
wharf in a nearby marsh where they could stand and
fish for minnows. Discovering this, their parents were
furious. At first, Benjamin felt justified because the
wharf was so "useful." Josiah "convinc'd me," Benjamin later wrote, "that nothing was useful which was
not honest."

Another time, Benjamin decided that swimming in
the ordinary way wasn't good enough. So he built a
set of wooden paddles to help him swim faster. He
also tied himself to a kite so that it could help to pull
him across the river. These inventions showed that he
was forming an important habit: closely observing the
natural world.

While Benjamin could be exasperating, his father
was proud of his curiosity and intelligence. When
Benjamin was eight, Josiah enrolled him in Boston
Grammar School. It taught subjects such as Latin that
helped boys prepare for professional careers. Josiah's

other sons were learning ordinary trades. But Josiah was a member of a church that was similar to a modern Congregational church. He wanted Benjamin to become a minister. As he explained, guiding his tenth boy into the ministry was a way of tithing (giving one-tenth of one's wealth to the church). Unfortunately, Benjamin was an unruly student. Josiah took him out of the school after just one year.

Josiah next enrolled Benjamin in a school led by George Brownell ("a then famous man," as Benjamin later wrote). And he began to reconsider Benjamin's future. To complete his son's education for the ministry, Josiah would eventually have to send Benjamin to college. Yet Josiah couldn't afford to do that. Besides, Benjamin didn't seem suited to the ministry. He wasn't devout like his Uncle Benjamin. To the contrary, he seemed to question everything. Josiah withdrew Benjamin from Brownell's school after Benjamin had received one more year of education.

Boston was then the largest town in North America, with nearly twelve thousand inhabitants. Sailing ships brought goods from Europe, the West Indies, and Africa into its harbor. They traded for New England products such as timber, fish, and rum, which they could sell in Great Britain. A man would always find plenty of customers for soap and candles in a town like this. Josiah decided Benjamin would join him in his own workshop, learning the trade of chandler.

From about 1716 to 1718, young Benjamin worked with his father as a chandler.

LEARNING A TRADE

Ten-year-old Benjamin helped to make candles by filling molds with wicks and tallow (melted animal fat). He also helped prepare soap, boiling tallow with wood ashes in a cast-iron kettle. The work was hot, dirty, and boring. It didn't take him long to decide he didn't want to follow in his father's footsteps.

Josiah realized that being a chandler would never satisfy Benjamin. Wondering what kind of job would suit Benjamin best, Josiah took him walking about town to see bricklayers, joiners, and other workmen at their tasks. Benjamin loved to read, so Josiah finally decided that Benjamin might like to work as a printer.

In 1718 Josiah sent Benjamin to Benjamin's older brother James, who owned a nearby printing shop. Benjamin was to become James's apprentice. This meant signing an indenture (an agreement that bound a young worker to a master for a set period). When Benjamin signed his indenture, he was only twelve years old. It bound him to work for James until Benjamin turned twenty-one. Not until the last year of the indenture would Benjamin earn a wage.

James showed his brother how to cast type from molten lead and how to set type in wooden printing molds. Benjamin also worked the big wooden contraption that pressed sheets of paper against the ink-coated type. Using this process, James could print posters, pamphlets, newspapers, and even books.

The printing trade was more to Benjamin's liking than candlemaking had been. He loved working with words. He often read for hours at a time, well into the night. Whenever he came across a new book, he felt an urge to read it and discover what the writer had to say. Benjamin also discovered new worlds through newspapers and pamphlets. He enjoyed nothing better than the lively arguments over politics, religion, and science that were being carried on by writers in Boston.

In November 1718, Benjamin wrote a ballad called *The Lighthouse Tragedy*. It was based on the true story of the death of a lighthouse keeper and his family. Although Benjamin knew his ballad was not great poetry, he thought he might be able to sell copies of it.

His brother agreed to print it. Then Benjamin took copies out into the streets. He was elated when he successfully sold them to passersby for a few pennies each. When Josiah heard about this, however, he cautioned Benjamin that "verse-makers" were generally beggars. Being useful and having skills that could earn a wage were more important than poetry.

The hardest part of Benjamin's life was getting along with James. "Thou' a Brother," wrote Benjamin, "he considered himself as my Master, & me as his Apprentice; and accordingly expected the same Services from

Benjamin Franklin takes his ballad The Lighthouse Tragedy *to the streets of Philadelphia.*

THE AUTOBIOGRAPHY OF BENJAMIN FRANKLIN

any quotes in this book come from Benjamin Franklin's autobiography. He began writing about his life as a way of telling his son about himself but continued when others urged that many young people could benefit from the lessons of his life. The autobiography, which covers the years up to 1757, can be found in many libraries and on the Internet at "Project Gutenberg" <http://www.promo.net/pg>. In the following excerpt, Franklin has become a vegetarian and cooks for himself instead of eating with the workers from his brother's printing shop.

> *When about 16 Years of Age, I happen'd to meet with a Book written by one Tyron, recommending a Vegetable Diet. I determined to go into it. . . . I made my self acquainted with Tyron's Manner of preparing some of his Dishes, such as Boiling Potatoes, or Rice, making Hasty Pudding, & a few others, and then propos'd to my Brother, that if he would give me Weekly half the Money he paid for my Board, I would board my self. He instantly agreed to it, and I presently found that I could save half what he paid me. This was an additional Fund for buying Books: But I had another Advantage in it. My Brother and the rest going from the Printing House to their Meals, I remain'd there alone, and dispatching presently my light Repast . . . had the rest of the Time till their Return, for Study, in which I made the greater Progress from that greater Clearness of Head & quicker Apprehension which usually attend Temperance in Eating & Drinking.*

me as he would from another." Benjamin, on the other hand, expected more indulgence. He wrote, "I thought he demean'd me too much." James could be harsh. Often the two took their quarrels to their father, who usually—as it seemed to Benjamin—took Benjamin's side.

In 1721 James Franklin started his own newspaper, the *New England Courant*. Publishing a newspaper was even more interesting than printing books. Each new day brought some novel event or exciting controversy, and newspapers carried opinions about all of them. Lively essays enticed readers to buy a copy of the newspaper day after day.

Benjamin was eager to write for the *Courant*. He knew his brother would never allow that, however. James considered Benjamin too young and too ignorant to write the kinds of articles he needed. Benjamin decided to write an article anonymously. Late one night in the spring of 1722, he slipped an article he had written under the front door of his brother's shop. He had signed it "Silence Dogood." Newspaper writers in this era often used pen names, so James wasn't surprised to find an article signed with a pseudonym. James liked the article enough to print it. In fact, he even advertised in the *Courant*, urging the writer to send more articles to him. Benjamin eagerly complied. He wrote many more articles as Silence Dogood and under other names.

Benjamin was sometimes "asham'd of my Ignorance."

He had had just two years of schooling, so he tried to educate himself. He bought any book he could afford and borrowed books when he couldn't buy them. He studied arithmetic books and books about navigation, philosophy, and religion. He worked to improve his writing by studying articles by good writers and copying their style.

One time, Josiah read an essay Benjamin had written, intending it for a friend. The two young men had been disagreeing about whether girls ought to get the same education as boys (in this era, girls learned social skills while boys studied academics). Benjamin's essay favored better schooling for girls. Josiah made no comment on this topic. But he did show Benjamin ways to make his points more effectively. As so often before, Benjamin took his father's advice to heart. He long believed this coaching helped him become a better writer.

BREAKING FREE

James and Benjamin soon found that the newspaper business had risks. Boston's leaders—and the leaders of Massachusetts Bay Colony as a whole—were Puritans. Their religion gave them a strict sense of duty. They expected citizens to obey Puritan leadership, and they tolerated little criticism.

Sometimes James Franklin published articles that seemed to ridicule or question these leaders. At first, they did nothing. But gradually they grew more and more irritated. When James published an article mocking them for being slow to round up some pirates, they acted. In 1722 the Governor's Council of Massachusetts sentenced James to one month in prison and told him he could no longer publish a newspaper.

The *Courant* could continue, however, if the editor wasn't James. Determined to see his newspaper survive, James asked Benjamin to become its editor. James realized that the authorities might consider his apprentice to be nothing more than a stand-in for him. So James publicly released Benjamin from his indenture. Then he and Benjamin signed a second indenture, agreeing to keep it secret.

Meanwhile, James was still strict with Benjamin. Sometimes he hit Benjamin. "Perhaps I was too saucy & provoking," Benjamin wrote. More likely he was too stubborn and too proud to tolerate his brother's treatment. As far as anyone knew, Benjamin was no longer indentured to James. Benjamin took advantage of this fact and announced that he was quitting.

Angry, James persuaded all the other printers in Boston not to hire Benjamin. With few options for earning a living in his hometown, Benjamin felt he had little choice but to leave. He knew his father would not give permission for that, however. "If I attempted to go openly," Benjamin wrote, "Means would be used to prevent me."

In September 1723, a friend arranged for Benjamin's passage on a ship to New York. Three days later, Benjamin found himself three hundred miles from home in a city where he knew no one, and with "very little Money in my Pocket." He found no work. So he

Benjamin Franklin sets out on a Philadelphia street as a young woman watches. He later learned that her name was Deborah Read.

pressed on to Perth Amboy, a settlement on the coast of New Jersey. Then he walked to the town of Burlington on the Delaware River, where he boarded a riverboat bound for Philadelphia in the colony of Pennsylvania.

When Benjamin finally reached the wharf at the end of Philadelphia's Market Street, he was dirty, hungry, and exhausted. With some of his few remaining coins, he bought three rolls of bread. He ate one, and then gave the other two away.

On his way through the busy city, he paid close attention to everything he saw and heard. One sight stayed with him for a long time—the sight of a young woman standing in a doorway. "She, standing at the door saw me, and thought I made, as I certainly did, a most awkward, ridiculous appearance," he later wrote. Benjamin was not bold enough to approach her, but he would soon find out that her name was Deborah Read.

Coming upon a small meetinghouse where some Quakers were meeting, he went inside. There the seventeen-year-old runaway dropped into an uncomfortable pew and quickly fell asleep.

A portrait of Benjamin Franklin at twenty

Chapter **TWO**

MAKING HIS FORTUNE

YOUNG BENJAMIN FRANKLIN AWOKE A FEW HOURS later. He asked advice about lodging and soon found a room in the home of John Read, the father of Deborah Read. And within a few days, he had a job with the printer Samuel Keimer. Although grateful for the work, Franklin could easily see that his employer had little skill with a printing press. He longed for a shop of his own. But that would mean ordering printing equipment and supplies from Great Britain—an expensive undertaking.

Franklin had written a letter to his brother-in-law Robert Homes, a ship's captain. Homes had expressed concern over Franklin's abrupt departure from Boston. In his reply, Franklin pointed out his good reasons for leaving. Homes showed the letter to an acquaintance, Sir William Keith, who was governor of Pennsylvania Colony. Keith was impressed. He called Franklin "a young Man of promising Parts." And the printers in Philadelphia were all "wretched," according to Keith. The governor was sure Franklin could do a better job.

One day, Keith stopped by Keimer's shop and asked for Franklin. Keimer was so astonished by the governor's unexpected appearance that he stared "like a Pig poison'd," according to Franklin. When Keith took Franklin to a nearby tavern to talk, he urged the young man to travel to Boston to ask his father for a business loan. Keith even gave Franklin a letter supporting the idea.

So it was that, seven months after leaving Boston, Benjamin Franklin returned. He wore a watch and a

Sir William Keith visiting Benjamin Franklin's printing press

fine new suit—signs of success in an era when clothes were expensive. Josiah Franklin listened to his son and read Keith's letter, but he refused the loan Josiah told Benjamin to work hard and save his money. If the young man had almost enough money saved by the time he turned twenty-one, his father would lend him the rest.

When Franklin returned to Sir William Keith in Philadelphia, the governor was not deterred. "Since he will not set you up," he told Franklin, "I will do it my self." To Keith, this meant recommending Franklin to wealthy friends in London. Franklin had only to go there. He could make the necessary contacts, obtain loans, and buy his equipment. In exchange for Keith's help, Franklin would return to Philadelphia and print pamphlets and perhaps a newspaper supporting Keith.

Over the previous months, Franklin and John Read's daughter, Deborah Read, had grown fond of each other. "I had a great Respect & Affection for her," Franklin later wrote, "and had some Reason to believe she had the same for me." The two young people talked about getting married. With Franklin planning a trip abroad, however, Deborah's mother advised them to wait. "We were both very young," Franklin pointed out, "only a little above 18."

Franklin was not only too young but also too poor to take a wife. He was determined to become his own master. After exchanging what he called "some promises with Miss Read," he sailed away from

Philadelphia on November 5, 1724. On board ship was a friend of Keith's who was acting as a courier, carrying a bag of letters from the governor and others. Keith had promised that letters recommending Franklin were included in the bag.

Seven weeks later, on Christmas Eve, the ship docked in London. But when the courier and Franklin rummaged through the mailbag, Franklin's letters were not there. Franklin was dismayed. "What shall we think of a Governor's playing such pitiful Tricks, & imposing so grossly on a poor ignorant Boy!" Franklin asked. The answer, he mused, was: "He wish'd to please every body; and having little to give, he gave Expectations."

Thousands of miles from home and adrift in one of the biggest cities in the world, Franklin turned to Thomas Denham, a merchant trader he had met aboard ship. Denham was adamant in his advice. He said Keith would never send the letters. Franklin could improve his skills by getting a job working with the expert printers of London.

Franklin was intrigued with the idea of staying in London. This huge city, populated by people from around the world, fascinated him. He quickly found work at a printing house, where he continued to write pamphlets on topics that interested him. He and Denham became friends. They explored the great city together, visiting its churches and roaming its streets. Franklin also met many writers, scientists, and others in coffeehouses, where Londoners gathered to converse. The months slipped by. Franklin wrote only once to Deborah Read, saying he was "not likely to return soon."

Then Denham made Franklin a business proposition. Franklin would work in Denham's business in Philadelphia, minding Denham's store and keeping Denham's accounting books. Once Franklin had learned the business of merchant trading, Denham would give him financial backing. Franklin could begin making trading voyages of his own and eventually become a rich man. Seizing this excellent opportunity, Franklin sailed for the colonies on July 22, 1726.

On the voyage home, Franklin made a list of twelve virtues. He wanted to behave virtuously: to work hard, tell the truth, save his money, and speak ill of no one. On a chart "for regulating my future conduct," he noted his successes and failures each day. He was so proud of his successes that he had to add a thirteenth virtue to practice: humility.

A PROFITABLE DEBATE

Franklin had been away from Philadelphia for more than a year and a half. He quickly renewed old friendships and comfortably walked the streets where he had once been hungry and tired.

He found Deborah Read changed. In his absence, she had married a potter, John Rogers. Rogers had then disappeared. Franklin "piti'd poor Miss Read's unfortunate situation," as he later wrote. To him, she seemed "generally dejected, seldom chearful, and avoided company."

Early in 1727, Denham died. His business closed, and Franklin went back to work for Samuel Keimer. By this time, Franklin had worked in London with some of the best printers and journalists in the world. A masterful printer, he considered his abilities greater than Keimer's. The result was argument. Out of patience with the young upstart, Keimer fired him.

Then Keimer won a contract to print paper money for the colony of New Jersey. The job involved uncommon skills such as the detailed engraving of copper plates. Keimer needed Franklin and asked him to work in Keimer's shop in the New Jersey town of Burlington. Franklin realized that if he became an expert in printing currency, he could eventually earn an excellent livelihood. He took the job.

In Burlington, Franklin made a new friend in Hugh Meredith, one of Keimer's apprentices. Before long, Hugh's father proposed that the two young men go into business together. Mr. Meredith would advance the money for printing equipment and supplies. With this investment, Franklin and Hugh Meredith secretly ordered the equipment from Britain. Soon after the New Jersey currency was completed, Franklin and Meredith resigned from Keimer's shop and set up one of their own in Philadelphia.

Not everyone agreed that paper money was a good idea. Most wealthy landowners and rich merchants kept their savings in gold and silver coin. Many feared this money would lose its value if Pennsylvania Colony issued paper currency. On the other hand, small merchants, workers, and newcomers believed paper currency would help the colony's economy grow.

Not surprisingly, Franklin took the side of paper money. To promote his views, he wrote and printed a pamphlet called *A Modest Enquiry into the Nature and Necessity of a Paper-Currency*. Then he distributed it for free. His arguments helped convince the members of the Pennsylvania Assembly (who made the colony's laws), and they voted to issue paper money. Franklin got the contract for the printing. This was "a very profitable Jobb and a great help to me," he wrote.

Through contacts he made in the assembly and through his skill, Franklin continued to win contracts to print new laws, speeches, and assembly proceedings. "I experience'd . . . the Truth of the Observation," Franklin wrote, "that after getting the first hundred [dollars], it is more easy to get the second."

Eventually Franklin was appointed official printer for the Pennsylvania government, and then for New Jersey and Delaware. The money he earned enabled him to pay off the debts of his new business. And people realized he had been right about paper money. "The Utility of this Currency became . . . so evident," he wrote, "as never afterwards to be much disputed."

THE *PENNSYLVANIA GAZETTE*

When Franklin opened his printing shop, Philadelphia had only one newspaper, the *American Weekly Mercury*. Its owner and editor was Andrew Bradford, who was also the colony's postmaster. As postmaster, Bradford enjoyed several advantages. He could have his paper distributed postage-free along with other mail. And he could include articles based on the latest news from Europe, since he was the first person to receive news. This increased readership, since colonists were keenly interested in European events.

Despite Bradford's success, Franklin became convinced that there was room for another newspaper in this growing city. Unfortunately, Samuel Keimer learned that Franklin was planning to begin a newspaper. Still angry with Franklin, Keimer decided to begin one of his own. The first edition came out in December 1728, but it wasn't much—just a single sheet, with little news of interest.

Before long, Franklin was writing articles for Bradford's paper, ridiculing Keimer's paper. Many people read the sarcastic articles, and Keimer's paper became an object of public scorn. Frustrated, Keimer decided to sell out. His buyers were Benjamin Franklin and Hugh Meredith.

Within a year, Hugh Meredith decided to quit the business and start to farm. Franklin obtained loans from two friends to buy him out. By this time, Franklin had turned the *Pennsylvania Gazette* into a newspaper that reflected his own wide-ranging interests. He wrote articles on the weather, the circulation of the blood, the causes of earthquakes. One headline read "On making rivers navigable." Well-written and expertly printed, Franklin's *Gazette* sold all over the city and in some neighboring towns. Franklin made money not only from the sale of copies but also from advertisements.

In the meantime, Franklin and Deborah Read had revived the "mutual affection" they shared. "But there were great objections to our union," Franklin wrote. Deborah's husband, John Rogers, might still be alive. If so, then Deborah was a married woman. Another objection was that Rogers had left many debts behind him in Philadelphia. Any new husband of Deborah's might be asked to pay these debts. On the other hand, Franklin felt an obligation to Deborah. "I considered my giddiness and inconstancy when in London as in a great degree the cause of her unhappiness," he wrote.

Another complication was the fact that Benjamin Franklin had a son. Historians do not know the name of the woman with whom Franklin had an affair. And they do not know exactly when William Temple Franklin was born, but most likely it was sometime in 1729 or 1730.

On September 1, 1730, Franklin took the step he had long been thinking of and married Deborah. She was a member of the Anglican church. Because Rogers might be alive, however, she could not be

married in a church. Consequently, the Franklins'
marriage was considered a "common-law union."

Benjamin and Deborah Franklin moved into a new
home at 139 Market Street. Little William also joined
their household. The twenty-four-year-old Franklin set
up his printing shop and the offices of the *Gazette* on
the first floor of the house. From a small shop next
door, the Franklins sold books and pamphlets; paper,
ink, and other office supplies; soap; candles; tea and
coffee; and other items. In addition, the shop served

*Deborah Read. After a
long romance, she and
Franklin were married in
1730.*

as a small, private bank, since Franklin often lent money to his customers. "Debby," as Franklin sometimes called his wife, "prov'd a good & faithful Helpmate.... We throve together, and ... mutually endeavour'd to make each other happy." Two years later, Deborah gave birth to a son, Francis Franklin, who was nicknamed "Franky." The Franklins had become a family of four.

God Helps Them That Help Themselves

As a printer of books, Franklin knew that the public was often hard to please. No one could predict whether a book would sell enough copies to make printing it worthwhile. A shrewd businessman, Franklin didn't take many risks. He looked for safe investments.

He found one in the form of an almanac. An almanac is a collection of facts that appear in a new edition every year. Almanacs in that era listed the time of sunrise each day. They predicted the weather, suggesting the best days to plant and harvest crops. Almanacs contained so much useful information that nearly every colonial family owned one.

Franklin began publishing his own almanac in 1732. As he had done in the past, he used a pen name. The writer of the almanac was supposedly "Richard Saunders," or "Poor Richard." In the first of Poor Richard's almanacs, Poor Richard's introductory words seemed disarmingly honest. "I am excessive poor," he confided. His wife expected him to make some money

POOR RICHARD

Below are just a few of many sayings Benjamin Franklin wrote for *Poor Richard's Almanack.*

Take this remark from Richard poor and lame,
*   Whate'er's begun in anger ends in shame.*

Haste makes Waste.

One To-day is worth two To-Morrows.

Keep thy shop, and thy shop will keep thee.

Diligence is the Mother of Good-Luck.

Have you somewhat to do to-morrow; do it today.

Do not do that which you would not have known.

Hear no ill of a Friend, nor speak any of an Enemy.

No gains without pains.

Pay what you owe, and you'll know what's your own.

A spoonful of honey will catch more flies than a Gallon of Vinegar.

Beware of little Expences, a small Leak will sink a great ship.

He that hath a Trade, hath an Estate.

A good example is the best sermon.

He that won't be counsell'd, can't be help'd.

Genius without education is like Silver in the Mine.

Glass, China, and Reputation, are easily crack'd, and never well mended.

Work as if you were to live 100 years, Pray as if you were to die To-morrow.

The noblest question in the world is, What Good may I do in it?

This illustration from Poor Richard's Almanack *praises the virtue diligence (a steady, earnest, and energetic effort).*

with this almanac, he said, rather than "do nothing but gaze at the stars."

Poor Richard's Almanack quoted famous writers, proverbs, and mottos. Franklin, in the guise of Poor Richard, also included plenty of his own advice. In pithy, memorable sayings, Poor Richard inspired readers to practice virtues such as honesty, frugality, and hard work. "Love your Enemies, for they tell you your Faults," he told readers. "God helps them that help themselves."

Many families bought almanacs but not books. Books were costly. The printing process in this era was tedious and labor intensive. In addition, most books had to be imported. Despite the expense, Franklin had always managed to buy books. He would almost rather go hungry than go without books. Well established in his business, he wanted to do something for the people of Philadelphia. He began to think about ways to encourage reading. Together with a group of friends in a club called the Junto, he began

The Franklins sold a variety of things, including books and paper, from this shop.

to develop a collection of books for people to borrow.

Members of the Junto and Franklin himself would also use such a collection. They already borrowed each other's books as much as possible, then discussed what they'd been reading. Often, the group chose a topic to focus on. One was "How can smoky chimneys be best cured?" To find a solution for smoky chimneys, the members of the Junto discussed scientific principles such as the way heat causes air to rise.

Franklin and his friends set up their library in a small building that also served as a museum with displays of fossils, rocks, and other curiosities. They donated some of the books themselves. The Library Company of Philadelphia, as they were called, charged a modest membership fee and used the money to order more books from Europe. Members could borrow books whenever they wished. People who weren't members could rent books. This library was the first of its kind in North America. Franklin later remembered, "Reading became fashionable."

Meanwhile, Philadelphia was prospering. People were busily trading goods with other colonial cities and with Great Britain. Many new homes were being built. Fire was a constant threat in homes and cities heated by fireplaces and lit by candles and oil lamps. So Franklin organized a firefighting company. As he wrote, "The Good particular Men may do separately... is small, compared with what they may do collectively."

Franklin, wearing hat, used his skill as a printer to educate people on many topics.

Chapter **THREE**

FRANKLIN OF PHILADELPHIA

IN 1736 FRANKLIN'S SON FRANKY DIED OF SMALL-pox. He was four years old. Years later, Franklin wrote tenderly of this son, "I seldom think of him without a sigh."

Smallpox was a common and deadly disease in this era. Doctors had just learned how to protect people against it by inoculating them with a weak version of the disease. But the public had not yet accepted the safety of this practice. Rumors flew in Philadelphia that Franklin had "experimented" by having Franky inoculated. In response, Franklin wrote a newspaper article explaining that his little boy had caught the infection "in the common way." He began finding out more about inoculation and educating people about how it could protect them and their children.

That same year, the Pennsylvania Assembly hired Franklin to be assembly clerk. As clerk, Franklin attended all sessions and recorded the proceedings. He wrote up the new bills that were introduced and the new laws that were passed. The job could be boring. Franklin spent hours doodling at his desk, barely listening to the words drifting by.

The job did give him new business contacts, however. The bankers and other business owners Franklin met favored him by buying advertising in the *Gazette*. Franklin was also hugely successful with *Poor Richard's Almanack*. With sales of ten thousand copies every year, *Poor Richard's* was second only to the Bible in readership.

About a year after Franklin became clerk, he was appointed deputy postmaster for North America. This was a royal appointment, and it carried a handsome salary. Franklin improved service (for example, he increased the number of days mail was delivered). At the same time, he began to trim expenses.

Franklin's new jobs helped him better understand Pennsylvania Colony's government. The real power was clearly four thousand miles away, in London. Years earlier, the king had made Englishman William Penn the proprietor (the founder and chief landowner) of the colony. Penn's three sons—Thomas, Richard, and John—stayed mainly in England. But they had inherited huge tracts of land in the colony. They also

appointed the colony's governor and instructed him
what to do. William Penn had given the Pennsylvania
Assembly the right to make laws. But the proprietors
could instruct the governor to veto those laws. The
longer Franklin worked in Pennsylvania government,
the more he chafed at proprietary power.

"ELECTRICAL FLUID"

Benjamin Franklin was a keen observer of the natural
world. On one trip to the Appalachian Mountains, he
noted that the layers of rock contained seashells. The
area must have been underwater sometime in the
past, he concluded. "It is certainly the wreck of a
world we live on," he wrote to a friend.

In 1743, on a trip to Boston, Franklin visited Dr.
Archibald Spencer. Franklin watched as Spencer carried out some electrical experiments. "Being on a Subject quite new to me," Franklin wrote, "they equally
surpriz'd and pleas'd me."

The next year, Franklin invited Spencer to come to
Philadelphia to demonstrate the experiments. Then he
bought some of Spencer's equipment. And in 1746, a
colleague named Peter Collinson sent the Library
Company a glass tube and instructions on how to use
it for electrical experiments. Franklin and the Library
Company ordered copies of the glass tube.

In this era, electricity was a strange force that people were only beginning to understand. Scientists
were trying to explain this force, but their theories

THE FRANKLIN STOVE

The people of Philadelphia spent much of their time indoors, especially in cold weather. Mostly they heated their homes with fires in fireplaces. But only the part of a room near the fire stayed warm. Most houses had many chilly spots and drafts.

In 1742 Benjamin Franklin invented a stove that could warm houses more efficiently. The Franklin stove was a cast-iron contraption that took in fresh air from outside, heated it through a series of vents opening onto a small log fire, and then circulated the heat throughout a room. The stove not only kept an entire room warm but also saved on firewood.

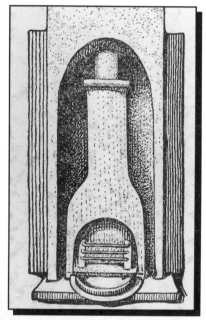

Benjamin Franklin's stove design

didn't satisfy Franklin. Franklin and others saw that certain objects conducted electricity, while others did not. Some scientists believed that different kinds of objects produced different kinds of "electrical fluid."

Several inventors had built devices to create electricity. One was the Leyden jar. This large, glass jar was filled with water or lead shot, then coated with a conducting material and connected by wires to a charged object. It could store a powerful electrical charge.

To start his own electrical experiments, Franklin set out the glass tubes and some Leyden jars. He observed closely as he sent electrical shocks through

Benjamin Franklin performed numerous experiments and proposed many inventions in his lifetime. This illustration shows the Leyden jar he used for many electrical experiments.

wood, paper, glass, and even his own fingers. He made his own hair stand on end. He set candlewicks aflame with electrical charges and sent sparks flying from charged and spinning globes. He made paper spiders dance between two electrified wires. He fired guns and rang bells electrically. He drew a crooked, blue electrical flame from the top of an egg. "My House was continually full for some time," he wrote, "with People who came to see these new Wonders."

Watching small electrical sparks reminded Franklin of something much more dangerous: lightning. Nobody really understood lightning, but many people had noticed that it seemed to act like electricity in many ways. Franklin wrote down a logical list of twelve similarities, including: "(1) Giving light; (2) Color of light; (3) Crooked direction; (4) Swift motion." The electrical flames in the laboratory could burn holes through paper. In a similar way, lightning could set buildings on fire. He noticed that pointed objects (such as knitting needles) drew the crooked blue flame even when held at a distance from a charged object. Lightning also seemed to be attracted to points.

Along with several scientists before him, Franklin guessed that lightning was a kind of massive electrical spark. But no one had devised a way to prove this. As Franklin continued to study electricity, he strove to make the connection between laboratory sparks and the streaks of lightning.

A Close Call with the French

In 1743 Franklin and Deborah had a daughter, Sarah. They called her "Sally." William, who had become a handsome boy, was about twelve years old.

The colonies were quickly growing. Immigrants from Great Britain and Europe arrived daily. Demand for printing work was growing. To profit by this trend, Franklin encouraged his apprentices and others to start printing shops in other cities, offering one-third of the money needed to get established in exchange for one-third of the profits. He slowly helped establish printing businesses throughout North America and the West Indies.

Franklin was an avid letter writer. He not only corresponded with friends but also with people who shared his intellectual interests. In 1743 he wrote to a number of his contacts, proposing that they all write letters to be circulated among themselves. This would speed the sharing of their ideas about science, philosophy, and other matters. By 1744 the group was established and known as the American Philosophical Society. A year later, Franklin organized a police force (or "watch") in Philadelphia. His corner of North America was becoming civilized.

At the same time, a war was raging to the north and west. The French and the British were fighting for control of territory in Canada and the western frontier of the British colonies. The French had gained the upper hand by recruiting many Indian nations to their side. In

Benjamin Franklin wrote letters throughout his life to share ideas with far-flung colleagues and to correspond with distant friends.

1747 the French sailed up the Delaware River and captured a ship about twenty miles below Philadelphia.

The war had drawn too close for comfort. Recognizing that Philadelphia had to be ready to defend itself, Franklin proposed that the city form a militia. "The way to secure peace," he said, "is to be prepared for war." But many people in the city were Quakers, and their religion didn't allow wars or other violence. For this reason, many people opposed Franklin. And the main proprietor, Thomas Penn, didn't want Pennsylvanians to form a militia he did not control.

In November 1747, Franklin published a pamphlet entitled *Plain Truth*, criticizing both Thomas Penn and colonists who would do nothing to defend their own homes. Then Franklin called a meeting of the citizens of Philadelphia. At the meeting, about one thousand men volunteered to form a militia. The number grew to more than ten thousand men over the next few weeks. Using their own weapons, the militia volunteers began training. They spent their free time drilling and target-shooting. They built

Benjamin Franklin created this metal cut illustration for his pamphlet Plain Truth.

walls and dug trenches to protect nearby farms and villages.

The French did not invade Philadelphia, and with a peace treaty in 1748, the crisis passed. Most people admired what Franklin had accomplished. Even many Quakers, "tho' against offensive war, were clearly for the defensive," as Franklin believed. Thomas Penn concluded that Franklin "had done much mischief." But Franklin was hugely popular, Penn said, and so "he must be treated with regard."

By this time, Franklin was forty-two. His printing shop was one of the most successful in Pennsylvania Colony. He had published books, pamphlets, the *Pennsylvania Gazette, Poor Richard's Almanack*, and the first novel ever printed in North America: *Pamela*, by the British writer Samuel Richardson. His wealth and reputation were secure. It seemed a good time to retire.

"SEIZING THE LIGHTNING"

In 1748 Franklin gave responsibility for his printing shop to a friend, David Hall. Franklin continued to edit the *Gazette* and *Poor Richard's Almanack*. He was happily left with "no other tasks than such as I shall like to give myself," as he put it.

Electricity still fascinated him. In 1749 he proposed an experiment to prove that lightning and electricity were the same. The experimenter would have to erect a tall iron rod at the top of a building.

The rod must be sharply pointed, since Franklin had noticed that "the electrical fluid is attracted by points." Then the experimenter would climb up to the rod during a thunderstorm. He or she would hold a wire near the rod. If the wire drew sparks from the rod (and Franklin believed it would), then the storm was certainly generating an electrical charge. A wax grip (or any nonconducting handle) could prevent the experimenter from getting a shock. A useful invention would follow: the lightning rod. Franklin explained:

> The knowledge of this power [will] be of use to mankind, in preserving houses, churches, ships, etc., from the stroke of lightning, by directing us to fix, on the highest parts of those edifices, upright rods of iron made sharp as a needle, . . . and from the foot of those rods, a wire down the outside of the building into the ground.

In 1750 Franklin expanded his ideas into a small book, *Experiments and Observations on Electricity*. Unlike many scientists, who wrote in Latin, Franklin wrote in English, using plain language that was easy to understand. His book was printed in Great Britain and also translated into German and Italian. A French scientist, George Louis Leclerc, published the book in French. He hired an English-speaking scientist, Thomas d'Abilard, to translate it.

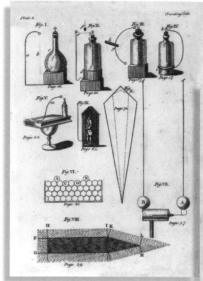

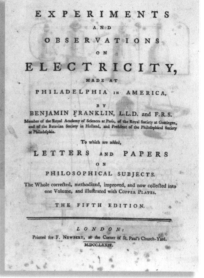

The title page spread from Franklin's book Experiments and Observations on Electricity

Intrigued by the experiment Franklin suggested, d'Abilard decided to try it. He had a tall iron pole erected on a wooden shed in the village of Marly la Ville, just north of Paris, France. Then he hired a French soldier named Coiffier to help him. On May 10, 1752, as a heavy storm passed over Marly la Ville, Coiffier bravely crouched at the base of the pole. He kept moving a wire close to the pole and pulling it away again. Each time, blue sparks danced before his eyes. Onlookers were amazed. Coiffier, d'Abilard, and Franklin had proved that lightning and electricity were one and the same. Reports of their success made Franklin an international celebrity.

FRANKLIN'S KITE EXPERIMENT

Benjamin Franklin is famous for using a kite to prove that lightning is an electrical charge. He never put the story of this experiment in writing, however. Writer Carl Van Doren reported that Franklin did read (and presumably approved) an account written by Franklin's friend Joseph Priestley.

According to Priestley, Franklin believed that his lightning experiment depended on an iron rod being erected on a very high place. No spire or rooftop in Philadelphia was high enough. So in June 1752, Franklin decided to use a kite to gain "access to the regions of thunder." (The experiment in Marly la Ville, France, had taken place one month earlier, but Franklin had not yet received news of it.) Franklin's son William, then twenty-one, helped him raise the kite during a thunderstorm. When Franklin "presented his knuckle" to a key tied to the kite string, he "perceived a very evident electric spark"—one of many shocks he withstood during his experiments with electricity.

Some people, however, debated whether lightning rods would really protect people. Lightning rods drew electricity out of the air and into the ground. The Rev. Thomas Prince of Boston wondered whether "Earth, being fuller of this terrible substance, may not be more exposed to more shocking Earthquakes." Besides, lightning might be part of God's plan. The Junto debated, "May we Place Rods on our Houses to guard them from Lightening without being guilty of Presumption?"

Despite the misgivings of some, many people in America and Europe began to erect lightning rods. Humans, livestock, and buildings were protected—all thanks to a gentleman from the newly settled continent of North America.

THE ALBANY CONGRESS

Franklin easily won election to the Pennsylvania Assembly in 1751. The assembly's only concern was Pennsylvania, but all the colonies would need defense if war with the French broke out again. Forming a common defense would require a united government.

Britain had found the last war against France expensive. It wanted the colonists to pay a share of the costs. The British also wanted the colonists to negotiate peace with Native Americans on the frontier. The Pennsylvania Assembly selected Franklin and three other men to attend a meeting in June 1754 to discuss these issues. Other colonies also sent delegates.

The meeting, which took place in Albany, New York, came to be called the Albany Congress. At the congress, Franklin presented a "Plan of Union," showing how the colonies could unite in the interest of self-defense. Franklin lobbied for his plan by publishing a simple cartoon by an unknown artist. It showed a snake divided into parts, with each part labeled as a colony. "Join, or Die," the cartoon warned.

Franklin's Plan of Union, the first ever proposed for uniting the colonies, was intended to strengthen the

When this cartoon appeared in the Pennsylvania Gazette on May 9, 1754, it became the first political cartoon to originate in the colonies.

colonies. Franklin believed Great Britain would also benefit if its American colonies were stronger.

Despite Franklin's efforts, the Plan of Union came to nothing. None of the colonial assemblies voted for it. They feared that any one colony might lose power in a united government. In addition, the British government rejected the plan. United, the colonies might threaten Britain's control over them.

Then in 1756, the French and the British again declared war on each other. Prompted by the French, Native Americans burned down villages, destroyed homes, and murdered settlers on the Pennsylvania frontier.

A battle of the French and Indian War. The horseback rider is an inexperienced young officer named George Washington.

The Pennsylvania Assembly searched desperately for a way to defend the colony during what came to be known as the French and Indian War. The militia Franklin had formed was a good start. But it needed money for arms, ammunition, and other supplies. The Pennsylvania Assembly decided to place a new tax on land, including the lands of the proprietors. When the tax law was presented to the proprietors, however, they ordered the governor to veto it.

Many colonists were disgusted. In 1757 the assembly asked Franklin to go to Great Britain as an agent for Pennsylvania. One of his tasks would be to meet with the Penns. Franklin would try to convince them to accept a petition from the assembly, asking them to pay taxes on their land.

French painter J. A. Duplesois created this portrait of Benjamin Franklin a few years before Franklin traveled to London.

Chapter **FOUR**

A MISSION IN BRITAIN

FRANKLIN SAILED FOR LONDON IN JUNE. HIS TWENTY-seven-year-old son, William, went with him. Deborah and Sally didn't join them, since Deborah was afraid of sailing across the ocean.

In London, Franklin and William found lodging with Margaret Stevenson, a widow. Mrs. Stevenson's fine house near the Thames River had been recommended to them by friends. Arranging meetings with the Penns and other British officials would take time, so the Franklins settled in for an extended stay. With Franklin were two servants he had brought from Philadelphia.

As the weeks slipped by, Franklin again found London to his liking. He made many close friends among the diplomats, writers, and scientists of the capital.

He sent presents home—china and tableware and tablecloths for Deborah and a harpsichord for Sally.

TAXING THE PROPRIETORS

For many months, the Penns refused to meet with Franklin. When they finally agreed to see him, they gave the Pennsylvania petition little heed. They argued that their power in Pennsylvania came directly from the king. They could veto any tax they wished. Thomas Penn spoke with "a kind of triumphing, laughing insolence," Franklin later wrote. Franklin felt a more "thorough contempt for him, than I ever before felt for any man living."

Unfortunately, a copy of this candid letter came into the hands of Thomas Penn. Enraged by Franklin's insults, Penn became his sworn enemy. "When I meet him anywhere," Franklin wrote, "there appears in his wretched [face] a strange mixture of hatred, anger, fear, and vexation."

Having failed with the Penns, Franklin began meeting with members of Parliament, Britain's governing body. He met with dozens of officials, trying to convince them that the colony had a right to tax the proprietors. Under pen names, he wrote articles for British newspapers. A skillful writer, Franklin succeeded in persuading many influential people to side with the colonists.

In April 1759, the Pennsylvania Assembly passed a bill to raise one hundred thousand pounds for the

FRANKLIN THE MUSICIAN

Benjamin Franklin loved music and played several musical instruments, including the violin and the harp. In 1761, while living in London, Franklin invented a new musical instrument, the armonica. Based on an older instrument called the Glasspiel, the armonica was a set of spinning cups. Its sound was similar to the sound made when a finger is rubbed around the rim of a water-filled glass. The best composers of the time—including Mozart and Beethoven—wrote short pieces for the armonica, and audiences flocked to hear concerts of armonica music. Unfortunately, the armonica was fragile, and playing it was hard on a musician's hands. It fell out of use by the 1800s.

colony's defense. This bill again included taxes on the lands of the proprietors. Surprisingly, against the wishes of Thomas Penn, Pennsylvania's governor approved the bill.

The Penns turned to the Privy Council, a powerful committee of British ministers. They asked the council to reject the bill. Franklin countered, saying the proprietors' lands would be taxed at the same rate as any other land. Their unsurveyed lands wouldn't be taxed at all. Reassured that the proprietors would be treated fairly, the Privy Council decided in favor of Pennsylvania. The proprietors began paying taxes on their American lands for the first time ever.

CALL FOR A ROYAL TAKEOVER

Franklin sailed for Pennsylvania in August 1763. William left London soon after, sailing for New Jersey. Thanks to Franklin's contacts, William had been appointed governor of that colony.

To people in Pennsylvania, Franklin seemed to know how to get things done abroad. He had even become "Doctor Franklin" when Oxford University and the University of St. Andrews—both in Great Britian—had given him honorary degrees. Franklin had been elected to the Pennsylvania Assembly every year he spent in London. He became the assembly's leader when he returned.

John Penn had become governor of Pennsylvania. He wrote to Thomas, blaming Franklin for local unrest. "While [Franklin] was in England there was at least an appearance of Peace and Quietness," he said in his letter, "but since his return, the old Sparks are again blown up."

In turn, Franklin bristled at many of John Penn's actions, such as offering bounties for Indian scalps. "All regard for him in the Assembly is lost," Franklin told a friend. Franklin and others began calling for a petition to remove the Penns from power. They wanted people in Pennsylvania to be ruled directly by the royal government—by the king and Parliament. Then perhaps they would enjoy more liberty.

But not everyone wanted a change to royal government. Some people attacked Franklin personally. They claimed he favored a royal government because he profited by it (after all, his royal appointment as postmaster brought him a handsome salary). Franklin was just another greedy and power-hungry politician, oblivious to the true welfare of Pennsylvania. In addition, some people brought up the fact that Franklin's son William was illegitimate. Franklin published a rebuttal to these charges. Nonetheless, after having served in the assembly for thirteen years, Franklin lost his seat in the election of 1764.

Unlike Franklin, many other candidates who favored a change in government were elected. Sentiment against the proprietors won out, and the newly elected assembly members voted for a change in government. In their petition to the king, they asked "that Your Majesty would be graciously pleased to resume the Government of this Province." Then they appointed Franklin to return to Great Britain with the petition. He seemed the best person to serve as Pennsylvania's agent in the effort to end the proprietors' power.

THE STAMP ACT

On November 7, 1764, Franklin embarked again for London. Deborah still refused to sail overseas, so she remained behind. Franklin again took lodgings with Mrs. Stevenson and began making his familiar rounds of old friends. He visited one high official after another, asking that the Pennsylvania petition for a change of government be heard. He also became an agent for the colony of Georgia, then for New Jersey and Massachusetts.

Many people in Great Britain opened their doors to Franklin. He was well known to important people, to scientists and teachers, bankers and ministers, lords and ladies. He spent his time walking London and touring the hilly countryside. He spent long weekends in country manors.

Few British officials wanted to be bothered with Franklin's petition, however. They were preoccupied with other problems. Great Britain had won the war with the French in North America in 1763. The French had given up their claim to Canada and to all their land in what later became the present-day United States. But the war—the costliest in British history thus far—had drained the British treasury. At the same time, Britain would have to defend a vastly expanded territory in North America. The number of British troops on the continent would need to be more than doubled.

In short, Parliament needed money. It expected that the colonies should share in the expense of defense. So, in March 1765, it passed a new tax with a law called the Stamp Act. The Stamp Act required colonists to pay for a stamp to be placed on legal documents and other paper products, such as newspapers and playing cards. These documents and products were illegal if they did not carry the stamp.

Colonists raised an angry outcry. They hadn't had a vote in the Stamp Act. Since they had no representatives in Parliament, this was "taxation without representation." In many cities, colonists refused to buy the stamps. In some cases, people threatened the agents who had to sell the stamps. So many people resisted the Stamp Act that it could not be enforced in any colony except Georgia.

These events took Franklin by surprise. At first, a small tax on documents didn't seem so terrible to him. Instead of opposing the Stamp Act, he suggested that colonists live more simply, so that they could afford to pay the tax.

Some colonists saw this as a betrayal. Franklin's partner, David Hall, told him that some even believed Franklin had helped to create the Stamp Act. This

Two of the British stamps colonists were forced to buy

Colonists in Boston protest the Stamp Act by burning stamped documents in a bonfire.

belief "has occasioned you many Enemies," Hall wrote in a letter. "I could wish you were on the spot, and yet I should be afraid of your Safety, as the Spirit of the People is so violent against every one they think has the least concern with the Stamp Law." Some people feared for Deborah Franklin's safety and urged her to flee Philadelphia. Instead, she stayed home, locked the doors, and kept a pistol ready. In September, a crowd of supporters stopped a mob from attacking the Franklin house.

The following month, October 1765, the colonists held a Stamp Act Congress. It declared that the tax was not the main issue. A larger question was whether or not Parliament could tax the colonies without their consent.

The congress demanded the repeal of the Stamp Act. In addition, colonists began a boycott of British goods. The boycott worried British merchants and manufacturers. It quickly became clear that the boycott was hurting them, and they, too, began petitioning for repeal of the Stamp Act.

All winter long in London, Franklin wrote newspaper articles defending the colonies and joining the call for repeal. In February 1766, he was called to testify before Parliament. He warned that if Parliament didn't repeal the Stamp Act, the colonies might begin an armed rebellion.

In response to these pressures, Parliament did repeal the Stamp Act. On the same day, however, Parliament also passed a law called the Declaratory Act. It proclaimed that Parliament had the power "to bind the Colonies and people of America in all cases whatsoever." The colonies had shaken off the Stamp Act only to be reminded that Parliament could pass another law like it at any time. As for the takeover of Pennsylvania by the royal government, Parliament refused to even consider it.

British "redcoats" march into Boston to enforce new tax laws.

Chapter **FIVE**

MORE TROUBLE IN THE COLONIES

IN JUNE 1767, CHARLES TOWNSHEND, A BRITISH chancellor, passed new duties (import taxes) on the colonists. They would have to pay these duties to import glass, lead, paper, paint, and tea. The reaction to the Townshend duties was anger. Colonists quickly organized another boycott.

No colony was more rebellious than Massachusetts. Its assembly called for united action by all the colonies. In response, Governor Thomas Hutchinson dissolved the assembly, forbidding it to meet again.

Anger over the Townshend duties and Hutchinson's response triggered rioting in Boston. One Bostonian, Samuel Adams, formed the Sons of Liberty, an underground organization that began attacking British officials and tax collectors. Adams's thundering

speeches inspired many colonists to demand their independence from the king. Acts of rebellion, rioting,
and arson spread throughout the colonies.

News of the uprising soon reached Great Britain.
This time, instead of repealing the controversial taxes,
the British sent troops to restore order. Known as
"redcoats" because of their bright red uniforms, they
patrolled the streets, guarded roads and bridges, and
began building fortifications at the city limits. Resent-
ment simmered as Boston was occupied by these
troops for the next several years. The Sons of Liberty
stepped up their sabotage, even burning Governor
Hutchinson's house.

The situation came to a head on March 5, 1770.
Some Bostonians began taunting British soldiers on
sentry duty outside the Boston Customs House. A
crowd gathered and began throwing snowballs and
chunks of ice at the soldiers. Nervous and cornered, the
troops fired into the crowd, killing five people. This
tragedy later came to be called the Boston Massacre.

Sitting in his comfortable London house, Franklin
felt a responsibility to smooth relations between the
British government and the colonies. Somehow, he
must persuade the British to understand the colonists'
point of view. He must also do something about Governor Hutchinson, who seemed to be losing control.

GOVERNOR HUTCHINSON'S LETTERS

Sometime in late 1772, Franklin was secretly given

some private letters written by several important men of Massachusetts, including Governor Thomas Hutchinson and his deputy governor, Andrew Oliver. Franklin opened and read them. They had been written in 1768 and 1769 to Thomas Whately, a member of Parliament who had since died. In the letters, Hutchinson had brazenly told Whately that the British government had every right to deny American colonists the rights enjoyed by other British citizens. "There must be an abridgement of what are called English liberties," Hutchinson had written. "I doubt whether it is possible [that] a colony, three thousand miles distant from the parent state, shall enjoy all the liberty of the parent state."

Franklin realized that Hutchinson's words would anger the people of Massachusetts. He also realized that something drastic needed to be done in that colony. If he could discredit Hutchinson so that a new governor could be appointed, perhaps peace could be restored.

In December 1772, Franklin sent the letters to Thomas Cushing, a member of the Massachusetts Assembly. Franklin asked Cushing not to publish the letters in a newspaper. Rather, Franklin wanted Cushing to show them to just a few members of the assembly. Franklin intended those men to use the letters carefully and discreetly against Hutchinson. Cushing tried to follow Franklin's instructions, but he soon lost control of the letters. They were passed from one man to the next until some members of the assembly demanded that the letters be made public.

In June 1773, the Hutchinson letters were read aloud in the assembly and recorded by the assembly clerk. Soon afterward the letters were reported in the press, which heightened public sentiment against Hutchinson. The Massachusetts Assembly quickly voted to petition the king. "With all due submission," the petition said, "[we] beg leave to represent that Thomas Hutchinson and Andrew Oliver... are justly chargeable with causing misery and bloodshed." The petition continued, asking the king to "remove them from their posts." The job of presenting the petition in London would, of course, fall to Franklin.

CHASTISING DOCTOR FRANKLIN

The Townshend duties were eventually repealed, except for the duty on tea. But the relationship between Great Britain and her colonies remained tense. News that Hutchinson's letters to Whately had been published in America only made matters worse. Gossip swirled around London. Someone had stolen the letters, but who? Some people suspected Whately's brother William and William's friend John Temple. Furious over these rumors, John Temple blamed William Whately and challenged him to a duel. The two men met in Hyde Park in London in December 1773. A skilled swordsman, Temple wounded Whately twice before the two agreed to lay down their swords.

That same month, a group of rebellious colonists gathered at Boston Harbor in Massachusetts. The duty on tea still imposed by Great Britain was intolerable. To make the point, the rebels slipped aboard three British merchant ships and defiantly dumped 342 crates of tea into the water. When news of the "Boston Tea Party" reached London, the British were outraged. Franklin was "grieved to hear of mobs and violence." He offered to pay for the ruined tea out of his own pocket.

Rebels empty crates of tea into Boston Harbor. This protest against the British-imposed tax on tea came to be known as the Boston Tea Party.

When Franklin heard about the duel between Whately and Temple, he decided to admit his responsibility. He announced in a London newspaper that he had sent the Hutchinson letters to Massachusetts. Many people in Britain saw Franklin's act as treason. Rather than condemn Hutchinson and Oliver for their letters, they condemned Franklin for making the letters public.

Hundreds of people attended a hearing on the matter on January 29, 1774. Alexander Wedderburn, speaking for the British government, accused Franklin of trickery and dishonesty and attacked the people of Massachusetts as well. He said Franklin acted as if he were the ambassador of "a foreign independent state." Franklin, who refused to refute the charges, seemed a symbol of American rebellion.

Thomas Hutchinson and Andrew Oliver were quickly cleared. Franklin, on the other hand, was publicly humiliated. He was stripped of his royal appointment as deputy postmaster of North America. William Whately sued him. Rumors flew that Parliament would try to prove that Franklin had committed treason. His reputation was shattered.

Franklin no longer believed that reconciliation between the colonies and Great Britain was possible. Yet he dreaded war. "I would try anything . . . ," he wrote in a letter, "rather than engage in a War with such near relations." He spent the next months asking for complete independence for the colonies. "Recall your forces," he advised Britain's leaders. "Renounce your pretensions to Tax us, [and] refund the duties you have extorted."

By this time, very few British leaders had any sympathy for Franklin's point of view. In January 1775, one member of Parliament proposed that British troops be removed from Boston. According to Franklin, Parliament treated this idea "with as much Contempt as they could have shown to a Ballad offered by a drunken Porter."

Not long after, Franklin got word that his wife, Deborah, had died of what may have been a stroke. He had not seen her for more than ten years. Clearly, he could do nothing more in London. On March 21, 1775, Benjamin Franklin sailed for home.

Colonial "minute men" from Stockbridge, Massachusetts, prepare for war.

Chapter **SIX**

THE SHOTS HEARD 'ROUND THE WORLD

DESPITE ALL THE TURMOIL IN HIS LIFE, FRANKLIN sharply observed everything around him aboard ship. He had often made notes on improving sails and ship designs. On this trip, he investigated a current of water that some seamen believed swept eastward across the Atlantic. By taking the temperature of the air and water each day, he found a warm current. He had proved the existence of the Gulf Stream.

While Franklin was at sea, British troops still occupied Boston. Feelings against them ran high. Many colonists believed they needed to be ready to defend themselves against the British at a minute's notice. Some formed "minute man" units (small militias) that began training and stockpiling weapons.

On April 19, 1775, British troops marched out of
Boston toward the nearby town of Concord. Their
mission was to seize a stockpile of weapons reported
to be there. As the redcoats marched through the
town of Lexington on their way to Concord, some
colonists took up positions behind rocks and trees and
fired at them. Marching in the open in their bright
red uniforms, the British soldiers made easy targets.
More than 250 of them were killed or wounded.

*Uniformed British soldiers fight the colonial minute men in the
Battle of Lexington on April 19, 1775. This conflict was the first
of the American Revolution.*

The British retaliated by burning farms and looting homes up and down the coast of North America. They reinforced their troops in Boston and prepared to occupy the city of New York. A British army in Canada under General John Burgoyne prepared to march down the Hudson River Valley to attack. Throughout New England, colonists hastened to form militia companies to fight the British. But with no regular army, they were outgunned.

When Franklin arrived in Philadelphia in May, he found the colonies surprisingly united in their defiance of the British. "I found at my arrival all America...busily employed in learning the use of Arms," he wrote. Years earlier, his Plan of Union had met opposition. This time the colonies were rallying around a common cause. "The Attack upon the Country People near Boston . . . exasperated the whole Continent," he wrote. "The Unanimity is amazing."

Almost seventy, Franklin had grown frail. But he believed in the colonies' right to govern themselves. He would do what he could to help reach that goal. When asked to serve on the Pennsylvania Committee of Safety to help prepare the defenses of Pennsylvania, he accepted. He also agreed to be a delegate to the Second Continental Congress, which was convened to conduct the war and to establish a foreign policy for the colonists. The congress met in Philadelphia just five days after his return from London.

The Second Continental Congress appointed Franklin as its first postmaster. Most of the delegates were quite young compared to Franklin. But he worked as tirelessly as anyone, establishing new mail stations and more regular coach and ship runs to carry mail along the Atlantic seaboard.

The Continental Congress made some last attempts to reconcile with Great Britain, partly at the urging of delegate John Dickinson. (A conservative man, Dickinson still did not have a lightning rod on his house.) Another delegate, John Adams, thought pleading with the king gave "a silly cast to our whole doings." Most of the other delegates agreed with Adams.

The British would not negotiate. In August, King George III formally declared the colonies to be in rebellion. "The die is cast," he said. "The Colonies must triumph or submit." Since the mother country didn't have "sense enough to embrace" the colonies, Franklin wrote, "I conclude she has lost them forever."

"REBELLION TO TYRANTS"

By this time, scattered bands of colonists were ineffectively clashing with British troops. Congress clearly needed to organize them into one army. It appointed George Washington as commander in chief. Franklin was assigned to help buy supplies for Washington's men.

Washington set up headquarters in Cambridge, Massachusetts. In October, Franklin and two other men traveled to meet with Washington there. Washington was trying to organize an army of twenty thousand men. To defeat the British, they must be well disciplined and well equipped. Washington asked for guns, gunshot, powder, flints, shoes, blankets, tents, clothing, food, horses, and wagons, among other things.

When Franklin returned to Philadelphia with Washington's requests, the job ahead of him must have seemed almost impossible. How could the colonists produce all these supplies for so many soldiers? They owned farms, not factories. For decades they had bought their manufactured goods from Britain. Congress had no money to buy supplies from abroad.

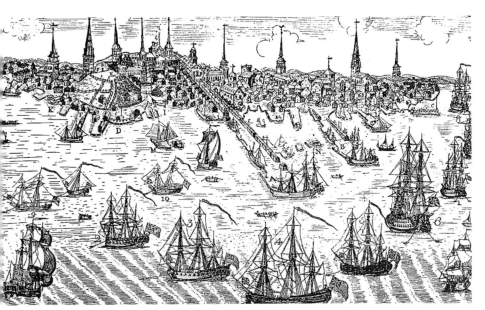

A fleet of British ships surrounds Boston Harbor.

Besides, the British navy was patrolling the coast, keeping merchant ships out of colonial harbors.

Clearly, Congress needed allies. Perhaps the French would help. Congress asked Franklin to meet secretly with a member of the French court who was visiting the colonies. But the French were not yet ready to anger the British by helping the colonists.

Franklin's son William was still loyal to Britain. In January 1776, Congress stripped him of his title as governor of New Jersey and put him under house arrest. Franklin had put his own life in jeopardy to fight for independence. Deeply angry that William did not join the cause, Franklin did nothing to help his son.

Congress continued the search for allies. The settlers in British-controlled Canada represented one possibility. Many of them were French, and they might be willing to challenge the British. In March, Congress asked Franklin to travel to Canada and make an alliance with the French Canadians.

Franklin set out with two other men from New York on April 2, 1776. The group made its way along the Hudson River and Lake Champlain to the Canadian border. The journey was long and hard. Franklin often felt ill. Heavy snow covered the ground, and everyone shivered in the freezing air. To protect himself from the cold, Franklin found a small fur cap that he wore for the rest of the journey.

In Montreal, Franklin's group found that British troops had abandoned the city and moved to a stronger position in Quebec City. Soldiers of the Continental Army (the colonists' army) stationed in Montreal were being led by General Benedict Arnold. The army was cold and hungry. Many of the men were suffering from smallpox. Under these conditions, Arnold could not pursue the British.

Franklin lent Arnold some of his own money to buy supplies. Then he and his companions met with French Canadians in the area, trying to arrange loans for the Continental Army. Franklin hoped some of the Canadians would be willing to help the colonists fight the British. Perhaps they might even fight to win their own independence from Great Britain.

The French Canadians had been well treated by the British, however. They refused to give assistance. When news reached Franklin's group that the British had reinforced their troops at Quebec City, they realized that Montreal might come under attack soon. The group could ill afford to be caught behind enemy lines and taken prisoner. They quickly left. Their mission had been a cold and miserable failure.

DECLARING INDEPENDENCE

When Franklin returned to Philadelphia, he found that many people were giving up the fight. The British seemed too strong, and the Continental Army too small and too disorganized. The scattered militia units were having no effect on fortified British positions. The British navy was sailing up and down the coast, bombarding ports and stopping supplies from getting through.

The members of the Continental Congress knew, as did Franklin, that failure would mean their own ruin. Somehow, Congress had to turn this small rebellion

Working together on the Declaration of Independence are, left to right: *Thomas Jefferson, Roger Sherman, Benjamin Franklin, Robert Livingston, and John Adams.*

into a full-scale revolution. Their best hope was to gain allies.

The French might be willing to join their cause if Congress formally declared independence. So Congress formed another committee and appointed five members: Thomas Jefferson, Roger Sherman, Robert Livingston, John Adams, and Benjamin Franklin. They would prepare a declaration that Congress could discuss and vote on.

Jefferson wrote the first draft of the Declaration of Independence during two weeks of June 1776. It proclaimed that the British king had taken away the colonists' natural rights to life, liberty, and the pursuit of happiness. It also proclaimed that its signers were forming a new country: the United States of America.

Franklin and the other members of the committee suggested some changes to Jefferson's draft. Then the committee sent it to the Second Continental Congress. On July 2, 1776, the congress voted to adopt the document with some changes. Two days later, on July 4, the congress accepted the final version. On August 2, Benjamin Franklin and fifty-five other members of the congress signed their names to the Declaration of Independence, putting their own lives on the line for the sake of a new nation.

This portrait of Benjamin Franklin was painted by British artist
David Martin and was later added to the White House
Collection of historical paintings.

Chapter **SEVEN**

WORKING FOR A NEW NATION

ON AUGUST 27, 1776, GENERAL WASHINGTON and the Continental Army were defeated by a much larger British force in a battle at Long Island, New York. The retreat left New York City open to the British, who took control of its busy and important harbor.

Despite this victory, many British ministers and military men realized that this war would be long and difficult. They had more soldiers than the colonists. But the colonists were scattered along a vast continental coastline. And the colonists were fighting in their own land. They knew the terrain. Instead of fighting in the open in rigid lines of troops, colonists made small-scale, guerrilla attacks that confused the British commanders.

The British also realized that victory in America would bring its own problems. If they won the war, they would have to occupy North America indefinitely, since the rebellion would probably continue to simmer. Maintaining control would come at a great cost. And America would only gain in strength in the coming years. Its population was growing larger all the time with new immigrants from Britain and Europe.

Not surprisingly, the British asked to meet with members of the Continental Congress. Congress sent Benjamin Franklin, John Adams, and Edward Rutledge as its representatives.

At the meeting, Franklin told the British that the colonists would agree to nothing without first having their independence. If Britain would recognize the colonists' new, independent nation, then the war could be stopped. The United States might even enter an alliance with Britain. An alliance of the two nations, one on each side of the Atlantic, would create a powerful coalition. The British Empire could remain the strongest and richest in the world.

The British representatives countered with a proposal from the British government. The leaders of the rebellion could be pardoned for their actions. Britain might end the taxes and other laws that the colonists opposed. But the colonies would remain colonies.

Franklin and his two companions listened, then politely left. The war would probably continue for a long time. They had one simple demand—complete independence. But independence was the one thing the British would not grant.

SAILING EAST AGAIN

In March 1776, the Continental Congress had sent a representative, Silas Deane, to France. His mission was to persuade the French government to lend money to the colonists. He also was meeting with French merchants to arrange the secret shipment of arms and supplies across the Atlantic.

Deane's mission was not going well, however. The French didn't want another war with Great Britain. They didn't think the colonists' rebellion was going to succeed. French aristocrats weren't even sure they wanted it to succeed. If the Americans defeated the armies of King George III, their example might inspire discontent with the French monarch, King Louis XVI.

Since Deane was struggling, Congress decided to send help. Again they called on Benjamin Franklin. He would be well received in Europe, where he was famous as the man who had discovered the secrets of electricity and who had invented the lightning rod.

Franklin agreed to the assignment. In October 1776, he set out with two of his grandsons, William Temple Franklin (William's son) and Benjamin Franklin Bache (Sally's son). Their journey across the sea was risky, since the British navy controlled the Atlantic. But no British ship stopped them. They landed on the western coast of France in late November, then traveled by coach to Paris.

WATCHING FRANKLIN

News of Franklin's arrival quickly spread throughout France and even to Britain. The British realized that Franklin would try to persuade France to give aid to the colonists. They protested to the French government, demanding that it expel Franklin. The French refused.

Franklin and his two grandsons are greeted by a crowd of French admirers.

When Franklin reached Paris, he wrote to the Count de Vergennes, the foreign minister of King Louis XVI. Franklin came right to the point. He wanted to negotiate a treaty of friendship between the French king and the colonists.

Vergennes refused to consider a treaty, since that would create a formal alliance that might further anger the British. But Vergennes didn't want to turn Franklin away empty-handed. So he agreed to open French ports to American ships, allowing Americans to trade freely with French merchants. He also agreed to aid American privateers (sailing ships commissioned by the Continental Congress to raid British merchant ships). They could sell their captured goods in French ports.

Franklin accepted these offers. The French still might be persuaded to sign a treaty, but convincing them would take time. So Franklin settled down in the town of Passy in the hills just west of Paris. He rented a fine old house that belonged to Donatien de Chaumont, a weathy businessman who was already selling arms to the colonists.

LIVING IN PASSY

Franklin knew that his mission depended on courtly manners, judicious actions, and tactful words. He had a sensitive role to play. To win acceptance among the French, he invited important people to dine at his home and accepted invitations to their homes. Each day and evening, he met with merchants, government

BIFOCALS

I wear my Spectacles constantly," Benjamin Franklin once told a friend. This often caused a problem, however. For example, at large dinner parties, "the Glasses that serve me best at Table to see what I eat [are not] the best to see the Faces of those on the other Side of the Table who speak to me."

To avoid taking his eyeglasses off constantly, Franklin ordered some specialized lenses with only the lower half ground to his prescription. The upper half was clear glass. Wearing these lenses, "I have only to move my Eyes up or down, as I want to see distinctly far or near," he explained. He had invented bifocals.

Franklin was living in France at the time. He found his bifocals helped him understand French, which he spoke poorly. "When one's Ears are not well accustomed to the Sounds of a Language," he wrote, "a Sight of the Movements in the Features of him that speaks helps to explain."

Franklin examines a sketch for the bifocals he invented.

officials, aristocrats, writers, and scientists, trying to persuade these influential people to support the American Revolution.

Over time, Franklin became a celebrity in France. People everywhere—rich and poor, important and humble— knew who he was. They recognized his face from the many paintings of Franklin by popular French artists. Hundreds of prints and engravings were produced in mass quantities that made it possible for thousands of French people to hang a portrait of Benjamin Franklin in their homes.

The French loved Franklin because he was an enemy of Britain, their longtime rival. But perhaps even more important, Franklin represented liberties that the common people of France didn't enjoy under their own king. Franklin's simple manner of speaking was nothing like the haughty airs of the French king and his court. Franklin wore simple clothes, not elaborate court dress. He seemed a friendly old gentleman, like a kind uncle or grandfather. Many people called him "Papa Franklin."

As 1777 wore on, the war in North America was going badly. The British marched on Philadelphia and captured it. They seized Franklin's house there and turned it into a barracks. The British also had spies in France who were following Franklin's every move. These informants reported on Franklin's meetings with French officials and even read his letters. One spy, Dr. Edward Bancroft, was an old friend of Franklin's who lived with Franklin in the house in Passy.

VICTORY AND TREATY

In the fall of 1777, the British prepared for an attack on the Hudson River Valley of New York. One British army would march from the north and another from the south. The two armies were supposed to capture fortifications along the river, then meet one another, splitting the colonies in two.

The southern army never received its orders, however. The Continental Army met the northern force at Saratoga, New York. Hungry and isolated, the British surrendered on October 17, 1777. The Continental Army had won a significant victory against the seemingly invincible redcoats.

The victory at Saratoga changed everything for Benjamin Franklin and for the colonists. Immediately after hearing of it, Franklin sent the news to every important French official he knew, including the Count de Vergennes. The French suddenly realized that this American Revolution might succeed. King Louis himself sent word to Franklin that he would listen to any proposals that Franklin might offer.

Franklin suggested an alliance of the Americans with both France and Spain against Great Britain. Although Spain did not accept, the French did. On February 6, 1778, Franklin signed three agreements with the government of France. The Treaty of Amity and Commerce allowed the French to give all necessary aid—including money, arms, and other supplies—to the Americans. The Treaty of Alliance would ally the

British General John Burgoyne surrenders to colonial General Horatio Gates at the end of the Battle of Saratoga.

United States with France if a war broke out between France and Great Britain. A Secret Article allowed Spain to join the alliance against Great Britain if it chose to do so in the future. The Continental Congress ratified these agreements in May 1778, and French arms, soldiers, and military leaders began to journey across the Atlantic to help the colonists.

The support of France turned the tide of the American Revolution. The British continued to maneuver around the endless continent, capturing cities and burning homes. On the other hand, the French sent their best generals and admirals to assist the Americans. And the colonists proved more worthy as combatants than anyone had predicted.

Lord Charles Cornwallis surrenders by handing his sword to George Washington in Yorktown, Virginia.

In the summer of 1781, a French fleet under Admiral François de Grasse sailed to the mouth of Chesapeake Bay. The fleet trapped a British army at Yorktown, Virginia, a fortified position on the James River. Washington hurried to Yorktown with his army. On October 19, 1781, after a long bombardment from both land and sea, the British surrendered.

Franklin, who had remained in Passy as an American ambassador, rejoiced when he received this news. The victory at Yorktown proved decisive. With John Adams and John Jay, Franklin began negotiating another treaty—this time with the British. The Americans demanded independence for the United States. In two treaties signed on November 30, 1782, and on September 3, 1783, the British and the Americans ended the war. Independence was won.

A Last Journey Home

By this time, Franklin was weary and wished to return to the colonies. But the Continental Congress asked him to remain in France a while longer. He realized his last years were approaching. In 1784 he wrote to a friend in Great Britain, "I look upon Death to be as necessary to our Constitution as Sleep. We shall rise refreshed in the Morning."

In May 1785, the Continental Congress sent word to the seventy-nine-year-old Franklin that his duties as diplomat to France were finally finished. Franklin prepared to return home. He packed more than one hundred boxes full of his possessions. On July 12, nearly everyone in Passy turned out to say good-bye.

Franklin sometimes experienced pain in his legs. Because he found it difficult to walk, or even to ride in a coach, he rode in a litter (a chair carried by two men) to the coast. Then he took a ship across the English Channel to Southampton, England. This time, he stayed in Great Britain only a few days.

Fresh off the boat from France, Ben Franklin receives a welcome home greeting at the Market Street Wharf in Philadelphia.

Many of his British friends came to Southampton to greet him. He met briefly with his son William, who had been released from his imprisonment. Franklin could not fully forgive William, and the two greeted one another cautiously. On July 28, Franklin sailed for home.

CREATING THE CONSTITUTION

Back home in Philadelphia, Franklin met old friends, carried on experiments, and played with his grandchildren. At night he enjoyed reading or writing and playing chess or cards with the many guests who came to call.

Franklin kept on inventing, even as his health began to fail and as his body grew weaker. He built a device to pluck books from high library shelves. He built a small fan into a chair to keep himself cool as he read. He built a clock and a device that automatically copied out letters as they were written. He installed a contraption that allowed him to lock his bedroom door without getting out of his bed.

Meanwhile, the new United States of America was making do with a government that dated to wartime. But a better system was clearly needed. In May 1787, a Constitutional Convention began in Philadelphia to devise a new system of government.

Pennsylvania sent Franklin as a delegate. As the convention's delegates bickered over the details of a constitution, Franklin watched from his chair, making

Delegates converse at the Constitutional Convention in Philadelphia in 1787. Benjamin Franklin is seated, bottom left.

suggestions and calming the arguments. One of his suggestions was that the nation's leaders serve as unpaid volunteers. Franklin had seen how a lust for power and money had corrupted the British government. He didn't want the same thing to happen to leaders of the United States. The delegates did not accept his suggestion, however.

They did heed his call for a compromise regarding the way power would be distributed. Some delegates thought all the states should be equal in power. Some thought power should be based on population. Franklin's compromise led to the modern-day system of a congress with two houses: the U.S. Senate and the U.S. House of Representatives.

A Rising Sun

The compromises Franklin suggested were only a few of many that had to be made while the constitution was being debated. As the final document took shape, the delegates still disagreed on some points. But to be accepted by the new nation, the constitution needed the public support of every delegate. "The opinions I have . . . of its errors I sacrifice to the public good . . . ," Franklin told them. "I hope . . . for our own sakes . . . and for the sake of our [children], that we shall act heartily and unanimously in recommending this Constitution." His wise advice gave a needed boost to the adoption of the new U.S. Constitution.

Throughout the convention, Franklin was frail and often in pain. He had had a long and useful life. He could face death with few regrets. As he wrote to a friend, "Having seen during a long life a good deal of this world, I feel a growing curiosity to be acquainted with some other." He devoted his energy to a new cause—the ending of slavery.

On April 17, 1790, Benjamin Franklin died in his bed at home. More than twenty thousand people from Philadelphia and other cities attended his funeral. Franklin was honored with speeches, long articles in newspapers, and the memorials of sculptors and painters.

Benjamin Franklin had arrived in Philadelphia as a young and hungry runaway. By his life's end, he had become one of his nation's founding fathers, a world-renowned scientist, and a beloved mentor to an emerging generation of Americans. At the Constitutional Convention, he had called the United States a "rising sun." His legacy of police watches, firefighting companies, libraries, an improved postal system, and countless other contributions and inventions helped the new nation shine indeed in the years to come.

A TIMELINE OF REVOLUTION

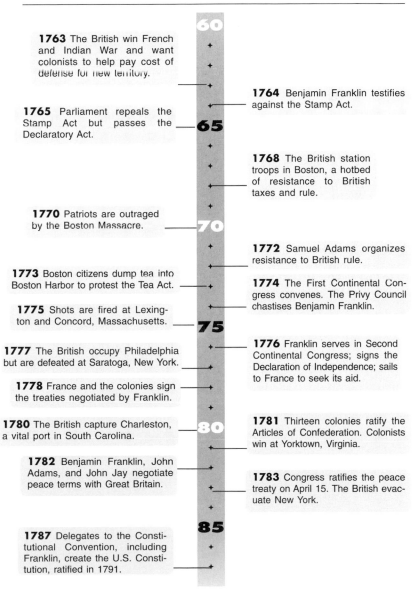

1763 The British win French and Indian War and want colonists to help pay cost of defense for new territory.

1764 Benjamin Franklin testifies against the Stamp Act.

1765 Parliament repeals the Stamp Act but passes the Declaratory Act.

1768 The British station troops in Boston, a hotbed of resistance to British taxes and rule.

1770 Patriots are outraged by the Boston Massacre.

1772 Samuel Adams organizes resistance to British rule.

1773 Boston citizens dump tea into Boston Harbor to protest the Tea Act.

1774 The First Continental Congress convenes. The Privy Council chastises Benjamin Franklin.

1775 Shots are fired at Lexington and Concord, Massachusetts.

1776 Franklin serves in Second Continental Congress; signs the Declaration of Independence; sails to France to seek its aid.

1777 The British occupy Philadelphia but are defeated at Saratoga, New York.

1778 France and the colonies sign the treaties negotiated by Franklin.

1780 The British capture Charleston, a vital port in South Carolina.

1781 Thirteen colonies ratify the Articles of Confederation. Colonists win at Yorktown, Virginia.

1782 Benjamin Franklin, John Adams, and John Jay negotiate peace terms with Great Britain.

1783 Congress ratifies the peace treaty on April 15. The British evacuate New York.

1787 Delegates to the Constitutional Convention, including Franklin, create the U.S. Constitution, ratified in 1791.

A Few Accomplishments

In Benjamin Franklin's long life, he achieved much more than any ordinary person ever could. He was an active member of his local community, Philadelphia, Pennsylvania; a printer; a postmaster; a political leader in the American colonies; an inventor; a scientist; a writer; and even a musician. Following are some of his remarkable accomplishments.

Formed the Junto

Helped introduce paper currency to the colonies

Published the *Pennsylvania Gazette*

Founded first circulating library in America

Published *Poor Richard's Almanack*

Founded firefighting company

Served in Pennsylvania Assembly

Improved postal service in Philadelphia and, later, in the colonies

Established the American Philosophical Society

Organized defense on the frontier and first Pennsylvania militia

Published *Experiments and Observations on Electricity*

Organized Pennsylvania Hospital

Studied and publicized population growth in America

Founded first American fire insurance company

Awarded honorary degrees from Oxford, Harvard, Yale, and other universities.

Served as agent for four colonies in Great Britain

Elected to French Academy of Sciences

Identified the Gulf Stream

Served in the Continental Congress

Helped draft and signed the Declaration of Independence

Served as ambassador to France

Negotiated treaties of alliance with France

Negotiated treaties of peace with Britain

Served as president of Pennsylvania Society for Promoting the Abolition of Slavery

Served as delegate to the Constitutional Convention

Invented the Franklin stove, lightning rod, armonica, bifocals, an improved clock, rocking chair, artificial arm, library chair, security mirrors, and many others

SOURCES

9   Esmond Wright, *Franklin of Philadelphia* (Cambridge, MA: Harvard University Press, 1986), 263.

10   Ibid.

10   Ibid., 270.

10   Ibid., 272.

10   Ibid., 269.

13   Benjamin Franklin, *Franklin: The Autobiography,* ed. by Daniel Aaron, with notes by J. A. Leo Lemay (New York: Vintage Books/The Library of America, 1990), 11.

13   Ibid., 10.

14   Ibid., 9.

17   Ibid., 14.

17–18   Ibid., 20.

18   Ibid., 16–17.

19   Ibid., 17.

21   Ibid., 21.

21   Ibid.

22   Ibid., 22.

23   Ibid., 25.

26   Ibid., 28.

26   Ibid., 29.

27   Ibid., 34.

27   Ibid., 36.

27   Ibid., 39.

28   Ibid., 41.

29   Ibid., 49.

30   Wright, 41.

31   Ibid., 37.

31   Franklin, 64.

33   Wright, 41.

33   Ibid.

35   Ibid.

39   Wright, 39.

39   Ibid., 72.

41   Franklin, 98.

41   Ibid.
43   Wright, 58.
43   Franklin, 148–149.
46   Ibid., 149.
50   Franklin, 109.
50   Ronald W. Clark, *Benjamin Franklin: A Biography* (New York: Random House, 1983), 144.
50   Wright, 56.
51   Ibid., 64.
51   Clark, 81.
53   Carl Van Doren, *Benjamin Franklin* (New York: Viking Penguin, 1991), 100.
54   Wright, 69.
60   Clark, 144.
60   Ibid.
62   Wright, 143.
62   Ibid.
63   Ibid.
66   Catherine Drinker Bowen, *The Most Dangerous Man in America: Scenes from the Life of Benjamin Franklin* (Boston: Little, Brown, 1974), 198.
67   Barbara Tuchman, *The March of Folly: From Troy to Vietnam* (New York: Ballantine Books, 1984), 165.
71   Clark, 230.
72   Bowen, 231.
73   Wright, 227.
74   Ibid., 226.
74   Ibid., 231.
75   Wright, 232.
75   Ibid., 230.
79   Ibid., 235.
80   Wright, 228.
80   Ibid., 237.
92   Clark, 314.
97   Ibid., 288.
101   Wright, 343.
101   Ibid., 346.

BIBLIOGRAPHY

BOOKS

Bowen, Catherine Drinker. *The Most Dangerous Man in America: Scenes from the Life of Benjamin Franklin*. Boston: Little, Brown, 1974.

Brands, H. W. *The First American: The Life and Times of Benjamin Franklin*. New York: Doubleday, 2000.

Clark, Ronald W. *Benjamin Franklin: A Biography*. New York: Random House, 1983.

Franklin, Benjamin. *Franklin: The Autobiography*. Edited and with an introduction by Daniel Aaron. New York: Vintage Books/The Library of America, 1990.

Lopez, Claude-Ann. *Mon Cher Papa: Franklin and the Ladies of Paris*. New Haven, CT: Yale University Press, 1966.

Lopez, Claude-Ann, and Eugenia W. Herbert. *The Private Franklin: The Man and His Family*. New York: W. W. Norton & Company, Inc., 1975.

Tuchman, Barbara. *The March of Folly: From Troy to Vietnam*. New York: Ballantine Books, 1984.

Wright, Esmond. *Franklin of Philadelphia*. Cambridge, MA: Harvard University Press, 1986.

WEBSITES

The Autobiography of Benjamin Franklin.
    <http://www.earlyamerica.com/lives/franklin/>
The Autobiography of Benjamin Franklin. "Project Gutenberg."
    <http://www.promo.net/pg/>
Benjamin Franklin: Glimpses of the Man. "The Franklin Institute Online."
    <http://www.fi.edu/franklin/>
"The Electric Franklin." Independence Hall Association (IHA).
    <http://www.ushistory.org/franklin/>
"Benjamin Franklin House" (in Cravan, England).
    <http://www.rsa.org.uk/franklin/>

INDEX

OTHER TITLES FROM LERNER AND A&E®:

Arthur Ashe

The Beatles

Bill Gates

Bruce Lee

Carl Sagan

Chief Crazy Horse

Christopher Reeve

Edgar Allan Poe

Eleanor Roosevelt

George W. Bush

George Lucas

Gloria Estefan

Jack London

Jacques Cousteau

Jane Austen

Jesse Owens

Jesse Ventura

Jimi Hendrix

John Glenn

Latin Sensations

Legends of Dracula

Legends of Santa Claus

Louisa May Alcott

Madeleine Albright

Malcolm X

Mark Twain

Maya Angelou

Mohandas Gandhi

Mother Teresa

Nelson Mandela

Oprah Winfrey

Princess Diana

Queen Cleopatra

Queen Latifah

Rosie O'Donnell

Saint Joan of Arc

Thurgood Marshall

William Shakespeare

Wilma Rudolph

Women in Space

Women of the Wild West

ABOUT THE AUTHOR

Tom Streissguth lives in Florida and works as a writer and editor. He has written more than fifty nonfiction books for young people, including biographies and books on history. His volumes in the BIOGRAPHY® series include *Legends of Dracula, Jesse Owens, John Glenn,* and *Queen Cleopatra.*